Lost Farm

Lost Farm
And Other Poems

ELIZABETH BOLTON

OREGON WRITERS COLONY
PORTLAND, OREGON 2001

© 2001 Elizabeth Bolton Literary Estate.
ISBN 1-891535-02-1

All rights reserved. No part of this book may be reproduced without written permission of the publisher. Reviewers, however, may quote excerpts.

Photo credits
Front cover: Barn photo by Robert Dittmer
Back cover: Elizabeth Bolton photo courtesy of Sue Bronson

Designed by Phil Kovacevich/Kovacevich Design
Edited by Lorna Price

Published in the United States by the Oregon Writers Colony
P.O. Box 15200, Portland, Oregon, 97293-5200.
Phone: 503-877-8072
Web page: www.oregonwriterscolony.org

CONTENTS

	Foreword: Remembering Elizabeth	7
I.	Views of Home	11
II.	Fabled Beasts	23
III.	Archetypes	35
IV.	Reflections	47
V.	Solitary Ways	59
VI.	Poets in the Agora	71
VII.	Antic Humors	87
VIII.	Time Gone	97
IX.	Envoi	107
	Afterword: Voices	111
	Acknowledgments	117
	Index of Titles	119

Foreword

REMEMBERING ELIZABETH

> Hail to thee, blythe spirit!
> —Shelley, "Ode to a Skylark"

My most endearing memory of Elizabeth goes back to one autumn morning a dozen or so years ago, when she drove down from her farm with a basketful of small, roundish blue eggs collected from the Aracauna chickens she was raising. She stepped in the door, blue eyes bright as her smile, hair windblown as the colorful scarf around her neck, saying, "I brought these for you. They're very low in cholesterol. When you told me you and Joe were fighting high cholesterol, I thought, 'These eggs are just the thing!'"

Some time later, I had a chance to work with Elizabeth when she became editor of the Oregon Writers Colony anthology, *In Our Own Voices*. I was co-editor of the collection's first edition, in 1983. I continued to co-edit the second volume in 1986. In 1988, Elizabeth took over as editor for volume 3. We communicated often as she dealt with computer and layout challenges. Amazingly good-natured, she worked dauntlessly on the project and produced a fine anthology. I was especially tickled by the inclusion of her poem "Catastrophes." Only Elizabeth could express poetically a philosophy that overrode one of life's demanding experiences— parenthood:

> When parenthood seemed too much pain,
> Think of my cat, who went insane
> When all her little ecstasies
> Grew to become Catastrophes.

Elizabeth continued her dedicated hard work for Oregon Writers Colony, subsequently editing volumes 4 (1990-1993) and 5 (1993-1997).

Poet, playwright, novelist, and teacher, Elizabeth's talent as a writer was as rich and varied as her personality. At ease whether writing an essay or a sonnet, she excelled in many forms, as the poems in this book readily reveal. One of my favorite poems is "Thanksgiving," which I read at her memorial service at Catlin Gabel School. In poignant lines, she describes her love of the earth and a deep tenderness for family:

> Chard rising lush in the snow was still summer green . . .

and later:

> Such goodness from the soil I labored in!
> Such great abundance for my paltry toils!
> The feast we eat today was grown right here.
> A miracle passed through my simple hands;
> Only my time and toil my gift to my family.
> All the rest is nature's gift to me.

Elizabeth's gift to writers of the Northwest is clearly demonstrated in her activities during her treasured years with us. She gave much time and energy to Oregon Writers Colony as president, and she promoted writers in other groups, including the Oregon State Poetry Association as well as in the community in general. She read on programs on OPB radio, judged poetry contests, shared her work at Satyricon, and conducted workshops at Marylhurst College. Among her many gifts, I consider her gift of self the most valuable of all. We salute you, Elizabeth!

—DOREEN GANDY RILEY
Poet, author, and founding member of
Oregon Writers Colony

The poetry of Elizabeth Bolton (1930–1998) attests more than 40 years of her writing. Some of her earliest poems, from the mid-1950s, are represented here in the sections TIME GONE and ENVOI. Most of the others date to the decades of the 1980s and 1990s, when she became fully engaged in the activities of the Oregon Writers Colony and other writers' organizations in the Pacific Northwest.

I
VIEWS OF HOME

Lost Farm	13
Requiem for a Cathedral	14
First Day of Spring (March 22, 1991)	15
Fog Zen	16
Farm Chores During the Drought	17
Thanksgiving 1979, Remembered	18
For Wiyanna (October 7, 1997)	20
Willapa Bay Before Dawn	22

LOST FARM

At the foot of a golden hill of ripened wheat
where another joins it, there's a cleft of green,
one friendly, fecund hollow, moist and cool.
Old trees shade the spot where a corral
held livestock. There's no power pole nearby,
but someone lived there once and scratched his life
from these dry fields. His house is buried here—
blackberry vines have mounded over it;
berried, too, is his barn. A chicken house,
perhaps, or a shed for tools, is over there.

I've driven past the place a dozen times
and still its enchantment holds, calling me in
to shove against a door on rusted hinges,
cross the silver-grey doorstep into the dark,
explore the pattern of the rooms, the life
that breathed here once, and went away, or died.

Machete work, to cut those ravenous vines,
or a herd of hungry goats, given a week
to munch the thorny leaves. I know what's there:
a place made special by the working hands
that raised it up before they faltered and fell:
no monument to power here, no shrine,
but a place once loved that wants to be loved again.

REQUIEM FOR A CATHEDRAL

There was a road wound steeply through the trees:
Three miles of switchbacks skirting a ravine
Where even in the sultry summer, lacking a breeze,
The cool cathedral peace made my heart clean.

Great trees anchored the road: even the deer
Would shun those steeps where mountain cats alone
Traveled with fearsome grace. Silence was here:
I drove with ease, muscle lay light on bone,

The ease of practice making this drive my joy
Until last month.   My road is clear cut now,
Awaiting autumn's rainfall to destroy
Acres of slash with vertical mud-flow.

A hot wind sweeps the hill, fanning my fears.
I drive, clutching the wheel, too grieved for tears.

FIRST DAY OF SPRING
(MARCH 22, 1991)

First day of spring; it's Oregon: it's wet.
Northwest of Portland on the wooded hill
The mist blows through the gap
That falls away to the west. Grey upon green
Blurs into grey upon grey. Out in the field
The animals move quietly, subdued.
I filled their water buckets, hauled the hay,
Portioned out the grain, collected eggs,

And suddenly hailstones hammered the barn,
Rattling down in deafening tattoo
On a giant drum of tin. The duck squawked
And hens ran to and fro. The horse shied,
Jittering under the calming touch of the brush..
I moved among them, finishing up the chores,
And lingered over grooming my little mare
As the barn cats stared impatiently from the hay.

This is the waiting time: the earth's too wet
For tilling. Seeds in the ground would rot. It's cold.
I'll spend the day in the den beside the fire
Shuffling words and smoothing them out again.
That's what the day is good for: thinking things out,
Seeing the thought, and then making it plain.

FOG ZEN

Parallel yellow lines float in the fog,
Dance to the left and right of me, and I drive,
A tightrope progress on the wild, dancing wire
Of the winding country road on the black ridge.

This is an exercise in Zen: The Now
Is all there is: the black, the lines, the car
And the bright glare of headlights on the fog.
There is no past: no future is assured.

My mind can rest in this, so sweet and clean
Are the intricate tiny moves that keep me alive.
No hope or dream, no guilt or poignancy
Survives my concentration on this dance.

At last the red reflectors shine from my gate
And I make the turn, and stop, and cut the light.
Time slowly returns, as when a child
I woke relaxed, innocent, to a new day.

FARM CHORES DURING THE DROUGHT

In the darkness, rainbows, even without a rain
Tears turning stars to gems that scintillate
Across the somber, summer-velvet night.

Daylight brings chores to do, laughter and pain,
And though I take small action, hesitate
Before too many choices, something's right.

Small unexpected talismans of love
Undo my fortitude and loose the tears
That blur all homely things to stunning beauty.

Without volition, I begin to move,
Knowing no hope, anxiety, or fears,
Taking each step without a sense of duty.

Centered in solitude, noting each need,
I raise my hands to nurture, and to feed.

THANKSGIVING 1979, REMEMBERED

> *. . . the house steamed with the scent of ham;*
> *There was candied apple, pickled watermelon rind,*
> *Jellies and jams and pumpkin pie and bread—*
> *There would be fourteen at table: all would eat well.*

Through the dense packed green of summer,
Weeding the dusty garden with the woods leaning close
Crowding my view, vine maple shading the orchard,
Water parsed out to the plants, weeds hauled away,

Through the haste of harvest, days growing shorter,
Potatoes dug and dried, heavy squash hauled to the house,
The green tomatoes stored to grow ripe in the dark,
Beans and peas frozen, all the fruits canned,

I waited for this day—a cold morning,
Clouds low and gray over the first snowfall,
Mist swirling up through the gap in the frozen pasture
As though sucked there all the way from the sea.

I dressed for the sacrament in warm boots and jacket,
Scarf round my neck and garden fork in hand,
Carrying a basket down through the snow,
Slipping at the garden gate, to the last green rows.

The one enormous carrot weighed two pounds,
Tender and sweet to the core. I pulled one beet.
Two parsnips came where I only intended one;

Chard rising lush in the snow was still summer green.
The snow was stained with the earth from my digging
As I stood and made my prayer to the winter air:

Such goodness from the soil I labored in!
Such great abundance for my paltry toils!
The feast we eat today was grown right here,
A miracle passed through my simple hands,
Only my time and toil my gift to my family,
All of the rest is the season's gift to me.

This is a holy day. The trees stand bare:
I see five mountains through the frosty air.

FOR WIYANNA
(OCTOBER 7, 1997)

It is cold where she lies alone
in that small high meadow,
the flowers massed around her place,
a new tree planted beside her.

A bright star is fallen:
in this child of field and forest,
heritage of two continents
now anchors us to that place.

Hidden under a new red blanket
that slipped off her high, sweet forehead
framed by a glory of sunshine hair,
she was carried up the long, steep trail

to the drums of her father's people
to the chanting of their voices
to the blessings of her mother's people
to the tears of all the people.

Spirits of the four quarters, earth, and sky
sweetened the day; voices, choked or clear
spoke and sang; gifts of parting filled
the plain pine box around and over her.

The scent of incense cedar and of sage
clung to us all in that clearing
under a dark, tumultuous sky
all afternoon.

It was done. When the first clods fell
the rain came.

I am not done weeping.

WILLAPA BAY BEFORE DAWN

There is a bay where dawn's announced by crows,
Where doves sound, patient and mournful in the trees,
Where gulls flock safely from a coming storm
And terns patrol the sand daily for fleas.
Grey silent herons stalk the tideland weeds,
Electric-blue kingfishers flash and dive
For stickleback.
                I can close my eyes right now,
Feel on bare toes the chilly, salty sand,
And walk the whole broad curve of bayshore beach,

And see the subtle coming of color to sky
Changing, as dawn approaches: purple and grey
Warming to lavender, unlikely green,
Peach-tinted clouds turning yellow and gold,
And then the brilliant reds that herald day.

The silver of the moon that glowed in predawn
Fades now, in my mind's eye, with the coming sun,
And every color fades away in fog
As the hot, inland summer air arrives
Swept with the great Columbia to the sea—
I shiver in these fogs of memory.

II
FABLED BEASTS

Caprice of Capricorns	25
Catastrophes	26
Christmas Elk	28
For Feliz	29
For My Filly, Dead	30
Red Vixen	31
Trapped Fox	32
Snowy Owls on Grassy Island	33
On Receiving the Gift of Five Peacocks	34

CAPRICE OF CAPRICORNS

A golden carpet floors the October wood:
Big maple leaves lie crisp upon the ground.
My goats are joyous, finding the season good:
They dance, break fences, kick the pails around,
Make crazy mischief, for they're wild to mate.
Their wagging tails flag readiness: they snort
And run like fools, bounce off the pasture gate.
Like deer and elk, it's time for them to court.

I'll board a billy goat for them next week
For hot times in the barn. The milk will sour:
Only when mating's done do the does turn meek—
Till then, they are Pan's creatures, in his power.

Autumn's rich harvests fuel my energy:
I race my goats to pasture joyously.

CATASTROPHES

If you think Motherhood a pain
Think of my cat, who went insane:
Most cats I've had would work and purr
And tidy up their sodden fur
And wash the kittens newly born
And stretch their claws and curl their paws
And proudly bask in our applause.

Somehow that cat seemed extra vain
Of her half-dozen little treasures—
Birthing's unexpected pain
Or the sudden sensual pleasures
Of six sweetly suckling kits
Titillating all her tits
Made that cat feel like a goddess
(We could see she wasn't modest).

While the kittens were confined
To a box, she kept her mind
But when these subdivided selves
Went scrambling up the closet shelves
Or played and hid beneath a chair,
She literally tore her hair.
She carried babies to her nest
When they escaped; she got no rest.
The kits grew large, her work grew harder
Dragging them back to the larder
Where she'd left a mouse or bird—
Things got out of hand, absurd.

Kittens do as kittens wish—
They ate the crispies from her dish,
They played and strayed: she, in dismay,
Grew more frantic every day,
Thinking the kittens part of her
Running amok, out of control,
She lost her soft contented purr
And howled like a demented soul.

I needn't tell you how it ended,
But you shouldn't be offended
At the lesson of this tale:
Mothers all, and fathers, fail
If you think you've made your offspring
Subdivisions of your self.
The illusion of your power
Lasts for its appointed hour
But to keep your mental health,
Let the children grow and play.
They will do so anyway!

When parenthood seems too much pain,
Think of my cat, who went insane
When all her little ecstasies
Grew to become Catastrophes.

CHRISTMAS ELK

Outside my kitchen window, in the snow,
Could I be dreaming shadowed Christmas forms?
Have Santa's reindeer come? Where is his sleigh?

I stood in awe, staring at live wildness,
Clean and healthy, very close, and real,
A herd of elk, a dozen cows and calves.

Graceful and calm, they browsed the sodden garden,
Pawed for windfall apples under the snow,
Nibbled alder twigs in the big brushpile.

In constant motion, without haste or strain
They flew, untroubled, over gates and fences,
Paused to play, as though planning to stay.

I stepped out on the porch. "Hello, you elk!"
Heads raised politely, stared, a little bored—
Who listens to an after-dinner speech

Unless the jokes are good? They understood.
Tolerant, they heard me out, and then
Went back to being Christmas elk again.

FOR FELIZ

White legs flash in the sun: the foal
Foolish and spring-giddy runs and runs.
Light and shadow dapple his golden skin,
Bright eyes flash: his nose, inquisitive,
Investigates: he tastes, snorts, and wheels,
Careening round the yard.
     Felicidad!
His name means 'Happiness'; he knows
What we, conscious and wordy, have forgot:
There are no words for joy. There is no way
To know a moment but through knowing it,
No grief that can be held, just as no joy
Will last, plan as we might to hold it tight.

To say that joy is fleeting, yes, Feliz,
Is trite. But so is grief if only we see right.

FOR MY FILLY, DEAD

Run, Lady Greylegs, in dream pastures!
Hold your head high and proud: flagpole your tail,
Roar through the woods and pastures, snorting and gay,
Leap over cars and fences: now you are free.
My love must not hold you here,
Nor my sorrow.
You gave me your trust, your affection;
You came to my whistle always.
I led you home from many a fool escapade:
I cannot lead you back from this one.

In tending and grooming you, I nurtured myself,
For I had forgotten living,
Forgotten affection returns:
Daily you reminded me
That even proud and free and beautiful
You could love me, seek my touch,
Follow wherever I walked.
You made it all easy and I won't forget you
Even when tears are spent.

And I will dare again
Because of you, my foolish filly,
Because of what you gave me:
Myself, whole, tears following laughter,
And a straight path in the morning.

RED VIXEN

Framed in a patch of summer sun, prick ears,
A little skull the shape of my Shelty dog's
Outlined beneath the shade of a maple tree.
"Look there," I cried, just as the fox leaped,

An arc of red through golden summer sunlight.
She ran like water flowing over the grass
Seemingly unhurried, with grace and certainty,
Too swiftly disappearing from my sight.

Six nights she sang, and then she sang no more.
Somewhere in the winter woodland, the fox curled
Deep in a den, her tail hiding her face,
A rusty lump of fur in rusty leaves.

In spring when frogs rejoiced, she sang again,
Hushing their jubilee with a new song,
A joyous song with lively counterpoint
Of puppy cries. Her song had been answered.

TRAPPED FOX

Do not cry out, oh creature in despair:
In your extremity, all help will flee,
Leaving you prey to all the ills that bear
A tooth or claw to wreak more misery;

And do not pray, for there is Justice here:
For fear and pain, pity is all you gain;
That insult to what makes your life most dear,
That pride in self, which you may still retain.

Courage and pain may still preserve your course
If you will gnaw to leave a limb or paw
Behind, as hostage to what's held by force.
(Help will not come: that is assured by law.)

Take no cheap pity. Look for no escape.
There is no pride that can't survive its rape.

SNOWY OWLS ON GRASSY ISLAND

Rowing the air with muffled oars, the owl
Swept silently over my head, so close
I felt the stir of air upon my hair;
Came from behind where I stood, checking me out
(What stood so still in his meadow? Was it alive?)
Before the moon rose, lit by the star glimmer only,
Thought I was harmless, went on his hungry way.

My eyes, seeking the stars of the Milky Way,
Were thus surprised by the black, inquiring eyes
In that little white ghostly face. Then came his mate,
Making her silent sweep over the meadow.
They flew to the trees at the far edge of the grass
And patient, returned, seeking the fat meadow-mice.
After they passed, I turned to follow their hunt.
There, in a snag, they paused. Was that a nest?

I moved only when they were behind me, slowly,
And came at last to stand by their nesting tree.
Discovered, I shielded my head with my arms; they dove:
White wings beating, beaks agape, talons,
Forced a respectful retreat. I loved them.

ON RECEIVING THE GIFT OF FIVE PEACOCKS

Marie de' Medici received no finer gift,
Despite her vaunted courts and lofty castles,
As this great peahen and her family—
Two cocks, two hens, nearly as large as she.

Not to discredit any gift of love, beauty,
Kindness, or gentle consideration—
I'm counting blessings!—for discerning eyes
Have seen my needs and answered them for me,

Yet this gift makes a queen of me, confers
An accolade, and in imagination
Crowns my humble barnyard with prestige,
Regal saunterings, and horrid cries.

Five peacocks, perching, make my house their throne:
No longer do I say I live alone!

III
ARCHETYPES

Synchronicity	37
Archetypes	
Grandfathers	38
Dad	39
Mother	39
Nanna's Hats	40
For My Parents	41
For Dad	42
For My Mother	43
For the Living Children	44
Hostage	45
Grandchild (for Amara)	46

SYNCHRONICITY

Great-grandmother Elizabeth,
Your picture is before me
Looking past my shoulder,
So I want to turn my head
To see what steadies you:

I have your curve of cheek,
Forehead and line of jaw;
Our eyes sit deep behind protective brows
But yours were brown as earth
While mine reflect the sky.

Your mouth is wide and firm,
Tight-lipped but approving.
Nothing you ever said
Hurt anyone, I'm told.

I know your secret, though,
Passed on in pencil in your book of psalms.
A hundred years ago exactly from that date,
I had a grievous day, not much unlike
What troubled you.

I read that psalm in awe:
I'd guess you never told a soul
Except for me
And God.

ARCHETYPES

GRANDFATHERS

My father's father didn't look like God,
Nor did my mother's father counterfeit
Omnipotence, though when he raged and roared
I didn't stay around to test his power!

My German grandpa's mansion was his dream—
Foundations, uncompleted, partial walls
And from the maze of concrete, one large room,
A kitchen, two small bedrooms, and a porch
Were all that grew. You had to climb a stair,
Traverse the nearly empty formal room,
To find the kitchen where life was, and warmth,
The smell of snuff, woodsmoke, and kerosene,
His coffee boiling on the little stove.
My grandpa's pants were let out at the waist—
He wore suspenders now, but still he sang.

The grandpa who was quiet had white hair
But nothing in him spoke of Power to me;
I can't recall his voice, or what he wore:
It only seems to me he never swore.

DAD

My father's gentle mischief made him my king.
On every childhood trip we took with him
Something occurred: one time he bought a farm;
One time we stopped at every ice-cream place
To savor all the twenty-seven flavors
In one day.
          He could anything
A man was fit to do, and do it well.
The king of mischief, then, but not of Heaven:
Beloved, admired, but not confused with God,
He did not think that he could answer prayers.

MOTHER

There never was confusion on my part
Between my mother and Divinity:
Brisk with propriety, she could be wrong,
And never read my mind, as angels might.

Hers was the softest hand I've ever known,
The quickest mind to certainties and plans,
And if I didn't fit, mine was the sorrow,
For she was sure I'd come around—tomorrow.

NANNA'S HATS

Out of an old fur cape from a rummage sale
My grandma made warm hats for all her men.
Grandpa never wore his hat. My Uncle Ben
Made a big joke how his might turn the hail
Or rain or gale, or even headaches' pain
From his bald head. My uncles Bill and John
Each thanked his mother nicely, tried his on—
I never saw one of those hats again.
But Dad, the son-in-law, gave her a hug,
Admired the curly fur, the foreign style:
"For a Russian prince, not of the rank and file,"
He said. She fretted: "Does it fit too snug?"
He wore it constantly, like a proud don—
It made me warm to see him put it on.

FOR MY PARENTS

There you are, at the airport barrier,
Unmistakable, squinting into the sun,
My parents, side by side, not touching.
I rush down the steep stairs into the wind of planes
And run to your waiting arms: hug you together,
Because we really have so little time.

Four children used to hug his home-come self,
Taking his hat, his briefcase, coat and gloves,
While in the supper-steaming kitchen
Mother quickly tidied up her hair
Because in a moment she'd be lifted off her feet
And swung aloft in joyous greeting.

When I made beds with Mother, homely chore,
She smoothed their beds with special, loving care,
As is her habit still. Always an early riser,
Dad wakes with the birds, makes her orange juice,
And leaves, beside the glass, the penciled note
She saves with others in her tidy desk.

We are all older now. We all have scars;
There were hard times, and broken dreams,
But this is *now:* The only time to hold a hand,
The only time there is to touch a cheek
To smooth the hair, to kiss away a tear,
Define each other's boundaries, such fragile shells
To hold the essence of a human soul.
So walk together gently while you can,
Not to possess each other, not in fear,
But to create anew what is most dear.

FOR DAD

Each time we part, it's harder. Tears threaten.
Words cannot pass the tightness in my throat.
Yes, I would take you with me—bundle you up
And ride away to wherever the future lies,
Tuck you both up in my knapsack, for it's cold
On the road I travel at night alone.
I shiver, and love is warm and nourishing.

But I will no more tempt you from your choices
Than I will abdicate mine. I remember your hand
Gentle and strong on the back of my neck one day
As we stood by the lake in New Hampshire. That touch
        sustains me:
You taught me racing starts, and set my feet
On the mark, ready to go, eyes on the hurdles.
Your hand on my neck was a balance, all my strength
Disciplined, collected, set on the goal.
I never lost a race: did I tell you that?

And now I am running again; no easy sprint,
But a long, hard uphill pull. I'm running clean,
Pacing myself at just below my top,
Taking the hurdles as they come, simply.
If it's "all in the start," as you once said, I'll win,
And if I win again, I've you to thank.

FOR MY MOTHER

She was the frame on which we built our days.
She filled our bowls with soup, our heads with law:
"It's time to sleep." "It's time to go to school."
Her censure was direct, her tempered praise
Measured our deeds and artifacts. No flaw
Escaped her eye: she was nobody's fool.

"People must stand for something," she would state,
And we would squirm, wishing we didn't know.
"You understand the point perfectly well."
Upright, meticulous, she held our fate
In strong, unflustered hands, and let us go
To dare to choose what we'd be proud to tell.

Only much later did I come to see
The elegance and laughter that we shared
Were not the common lot. The rectitude
That so obscured her casual symmetry,
Mischief, and grace, the lilting song she aired,
Allowed us nothing that was mean or crude.

FOR THE LIVING CHILDREN

I celebrate you, my son, my daughter, my son:
You shared the shelter of my flesh, but so did others.
Three lodged too briefly, fled before formed,
Till one dared stay to make Mother of me,
And three more tried, but found me arduous.
Then Child-of-Dream was joined by Child-of-Will,
And Child-of-Loving came with simplicity.
Though others came, also came starving days:
Only the finest three trained under my heart,
Rode my adventures, swam in my sea of song.
Buoyant and tough, tender and beautiful,
I wonder at you now, and what I owe.

I can, I see, open my shielding doors
To let you go, as once I did before,
With joyous song, thanksgiving, bon voyage,
And may we meet to tell our travelers' tales
And share a feast, a fireside, now and then,
And may you not grieve, as I do not, what's lost,
For in your bones, you know what living cost.

HOSTAGE

Life holds me hostage: two beloved sons,
A precious daughter, travel the roads tonight,
Each one is, more than I am, gifted with light,
Experience beyond a mother's sermons.

Each time we part my anxious prayers follow
The unknown roads they take; my eyes mist.
Remembering the tender lips I kissed,
I hold their loving warm in my heart's hollow,
As once I carried each beneath my breast
And sang encouragement to his unique
Being, blessing the path each one would seek,
So different in time to come, none best.

So have I parted from my parents, time
After time, wondering was this the last,
Since time, which blesses us, can also blast
Our human loves. It surely is no crime

Or sin against my faith, my certainty
That all is ordered, that the lively seed
Of future outcomes lies in every deed:
I'm no more trapped by them than they by me.

GRANDCHILD
(FOR AMARA)

Blissed out
as the children say
the child's small head
resting against my cheek.
Once familiar
was this soft weight
of infant weariness
nestled warm against me.
Ah, the sweetness
of that trust.
She will never be
more seductive.

IV
REFLECTIONS

Epiphany	49
Peace	50
Solitude and Purpose	51
Breakthrough	52
First Things	54
Deposition	55
The Logic of the Heart	56
Unmeeting Wishes	57
Of Thought and Reality	58

EPIPHANY

Death touched unwilling flesh, and left the bone
To show my structure. Finally alone,
Accepting humbly what no doctor said,
I saw the mirror opposite my bed:
Awake, I could not turn my eyes away
But had to lie and watch my face all day
And meet my essence in those shadowed eyes
That met my own, but would not sympathize.
Immobile, patient, curious and still,
I watched the first awakening of my will.

PEACE

Peace isn't quiet: nothing but death is still,
No noun remains itself: place, person, thing
Dance through their changes each in its different time,
Some slow as silence (so our mortal eyes
Perceive no change at all), some swift as love.

Needs replace fullness: rocks revert to sand,
What most seems certainty's certain to change
And nothing's true but reverence, nothing but loving.
Each moment's joy is "now": miraculous,
And to accept the paradox of peace is this:

To go and come as we must, trusting the time;
To give what we have and are without a plan
And yet to dare and plan, risk all and fail,
Grieve and rejoice, admit mistakes and laugh,
Admit we've won! and grasp to our hearts the prize,
Knowing we'll see it change, trusting the law:
We only guess perfection through a flaw.

SOLITUDE AND PURPOSE

All right, Universe, I stride among your stars
Treading the void as though a firmament,
Moving steadily, swinging along, singing,
Finding at footfall rocks of certainty
As though there were a road, as though a goal
Purposed my going thus—but to what end?

All right, Universe! My bare toes grip the clay
Of this one world among your myriads.
Naked, hot in the sun, I dig and hoe,
Plant seeds, pull weeds among the fruiting vines.
Rivers rise on my skin, drip from my chin,
Course down my breasts as I stand to clean my hands,

Survey the mark I've made, and call it good.
Perhaps I'll harvest here, reap what I've sown,
Or other hands may strip the heavy vines.
I plant and tend, touch a life here or there.
Who knows the outcome? Who can foretell the ends?
This garden place, or any place I stand—

(All right, Universe!)—each is my own.
Earth on my hands, mudsmear on face and thigh
Will wash away, leave me anonymous
To meet tomorrow with a morning smile,
To dig and sweat, plant what it is I am
in my new/old, never-and-always home.

BREAKTHROUGH

1.

White fields fade to snow-encumbered sky
And all is space, for nothing stops the eye.
The black road leads ahead somewhere: alone
I drive the black road, going somewhere, home,
Where, under snow, somewhere, my small dog lies.
I weep his once-warmth, his once-loving eyes,
That steady gaze that praised my every move.
This is not new: I weep the loss of love.

Speaking releases pain: these words, aloud,
Loose tears I had not shed. Pain is not proud,
But solitary, seeking not to grieve
Those intimates whose words will not relieve.

2.

White fields fade to winter sky, and now
The hiss and sizzle of the falling snow.
The black road vanishes, blinding my sight
As fast flakes hiss, and cease. Out of the white
A distant farm emerges, pale and grey;
The road returns to black, pointing a way.
In a stark tree, a hawk watches me pass by;
Doves move on a roadside fence, but do not fly.

At road edge in a golden stand of weed
A brilliant pheasant gleans for scattered seed,
Vivid against the snow. What can I glean
From white immensity?
                       I grow serene....

3.

Somehow my storm is still. There is no change
That does not bring its just measure of pain.
Like birds blown by the blast of inner storm,
We seek the seeds of life, a place that's warm,
We move, migrate. Claremont to Monterey,
Claremont again, and then Willapa Bay.
In chilly northlands we have raised our young
In the first lust of youth: now this is done.

Like birds, now that the young have grown and gone
We are alone. Shall we grow pale and wan,
Let storm winds blow us off to die apart,
Or shall we share what warmth lies in the heart?

FIRST THINGS

First things are always lost: first love will die,
The first big win, the battle you survived
Is done.
          The first child thrust into the world
Will be the first to grow and go away,
For Mother-havens turn to prison walls,
The Father-hero, challenged, overthrown,
Leaves you defenseless, shivering, alone,
Having yourself slaughtered your own innocence.

First things are doomed: they never come again,
But what remains after the newness goes
Contains in it all of our history,
Makes us ourselves: the sum of what we've lost,
And we can learn to see the present "new,"
And every day dawns Eden, tart and true.

DEPOSITION

We're all a little paranoid, I think:
For none of us is good enough, is tough
Enough, is brave enough to wink at God
And share His tolerance of all the sins
My neighbors have committed, not to speak
Of all the ways I know that I am weak
And not immortal after all.
                             Pleading
My case before the jury of my peer
(Myself), I know that heaven's gentler.
Though all the testimony raised by those
Who'd like to see me down is true, all right,
It's off the mark. Guilty of taking joy,
Shoplifting beauty from the everyday,
Daring to laugh where angels fear to play,
Why, all of that is true enough, I guess:
I readily confess it. Heaven has blinked
And let me keep the treasures I've amassed,
But I'll be held for this sin at the last:

I've failed of greed. I never learned to ask,
To beg, weep, and insist on one joy more,
Value what heaven made of me, demand
Its due. Bedrugged by homemade happiness
I need to wake at last, to make amends,
To ask the gift that dignifies the Giver:
Everything He is, and nothing less,
For only thus can He be manifest.

THE LOGIC OF THE HEART

The logic of the heart leaves much to hope,
And much to be desired. It cannot scheme:
Its plans are vain and hazardous; they grope
Through fogs, they do not build a path. They dream.

The heart is hopelessly impractical,
Wants what it wants, and will not be denied;
Stormy and childish, cannot wait at all,
Breaks easily, or puffs itself with pride.

The language of the heart is quite absurd:
Both tentative and unmistakable.
It offers everything without a word
But cannot lie, or tell a useful fable.

My eyes, naked, meet your naked eyes
And learn that laughter's better than being wise.

UNMEETING WISHES

I can see no other man, my love,
While I let you fill my eye.
I would not change a hair of you
So now must say goodbye.

And you may keep your heart your own
Or give it quite away—
For friendship's sake, and nothing more,
A little while I'll stay.

But I've a heart and a life to share,
And gifts to give and gain.
I'll see you off on your special quest
And turn to my own again.

OF THOUGHT AND REALITY

Distracted by a hummingbird,
A falling leaf, a missing word,
I sat, and knew the touch of spring
And had no further need to sing.

Thus tortured thought made its escape:
So life avoids intended rape!
Meaning remains in bird and tree,
Admired, but still a mystery.

V
SOLITARY WAYS

Winter Song	61
Deserted Wife	62
Dead Crow by the Roadside	63
Hill Farm	65
Skyline Drive—Sunset	66
Thanksgiving Meditation, 1983	67
Fall With No Harvest	68
Restless	69
Dark Day	70

WINTER SONG

There comes a time of solitude when one
Is strong: when wrongs storm the world around
While, walking fearlessly upon the fire,
One is exempt from every dark desire.
Frozen, a waterfall makes no hard sound,
Silent a little time beneath the sun.

But spring does come to free a frozen stream—
Nothing is still for long—and inner peace
Yields to its change as every natural thing:
Bare trees grow blurred with spring. Returned birds sing.
Without its leaves, the maple did not cease!
One is required to wake from every dream.

DESERTED WIFE

As an old crow, come to the season's end,
I rummage my tattered nest for shards of shell.
Those sparks of feisty life I warmed to shell-burst,
Wing-sheltered till the feathers came,
Grew loud and gay, ate hearty, learned to fly,
And now are flown.
                          Where is my mate? We two
Have raised more than this brood of gallant young
Through many seasons' sun and wind and rain.

Disconsolate, I clean the nest of shit.
The sun is warm today, the high winds call:
It's time to make our flight, to work the wings,
To fly and fly, and then, again, to build.

Where is my mate? What wind swept him away?
What can I build or nurture here alone?
His was the only seed I'd thought I'd need,
His wing against me was my only home.

DEAD CROW BY THE ROADSIDE

He lies upended, twiglike legs like trees,
His glossy feathers tangled and askew:
God's garbageman, who once patrolled the road
Too zealously, struck down by a passing car.

My job description's not so clear as his
Or as it was: I've done what nature bid,
Not so much crow as salmon, swimming upstream
To nest and spawn, defend the fingerlings
Against the hunger of my starveling mate.

Battered and torn, I float down the long river,
Surprised to find that I can see and hear,
Surprised to find I feel, as not before,
Surprised to note that keening in my ears
Is mine, is my own voice. Like Orpheus
Returned from Hades, I have tales to tell
But must consider how to tell, and whom.

Perhaps it's not my job to sing at all,
My hoarse voice cawing warning to the flock,
Irreverent and angry at my fate
Or making naughty jokes at Life's expense;
Perhaps I'm not as simple as a crow,

For crows will mate for life, as once did I,
Sharing my warmth in the nest, my busy hands
Combing the glossy blackness of his hair.

And since I'm still alive, and ever stronger
So spring tide energies hurry my blood.
It is no salmon-woman singing in me!
I have no spirit name, like Indians,
Linking me to the beasts: not fish nor crow,
Not wise coyote, or the cedar tree
But something new, twice-born, a child again
Trying my voice, my eager limbs . . . my heart.

HILL FARM

Once the long drive was painful: going home
Meant leaving light and comfort for a hard place,
Meant worse-than-solitude in a cold bed.
Only the warmth of children, love returned
As fast as given away, could warm those days.

There are no children now: I return alone
To a place that's my own place, empty and clean.
The bruises heal, the torn flesh of my heart
Has the clean ache of mending. Tears are not scorned
And laughter grows to lighten the darkest days.

Even the winter's ice is not so bitter
As the intent to injure. In the dark house
I'll light a lamp, build a fire, singing,
Work till the work is finished, go to sleep.
Waking to beauty, I wake to the work or love
Building each day, this place, my self, my name,
And when I'm away, I feel the strong, sweet call
Of the road that is my own, that leads me home.

SKYLINE DRIVE—SUNSET

Red barn against a cold and sullen sky
Catching the sun's last flame before the dark,
Strikes with its warmth not the material eye
Alone, but colors deep into the mind and heart.

What is this subtle sensing we call 'sight,'
Taking the wavering rays into the brain
To translate into 'beauty' or 'delight'
To heighten or contrast our joy or pain?

Empty, alone, but with a glass of sherry
Against the body's needs, I take the roads
With ease. The challenges and turns make merry
Rhythms, syncopate what sight implodes.

Teasing each sense with taste of ecstacy:
As I drive the edge of death, The World courts me.

THANKSGIVING MEDITATION, 1983

Early, restless, I slip from the sleeping house
To drive the dark ridge road before the dawn.
Somewhere under lowering clouds must be a moon:
The wet road gleams under black trees ahead.
I use no lights: quiet, the car purrs
Like a secret, small gold cat prowling the night,
Its eyes alert, but dark, reflect no light.

Unpeopled at this hour, the world is mine,
Its forms defined, tree and barn outlined
Softly against the sky. I reach the height:
Below me, sleeping towns and city lie.
The city lights cover the valley floors
Studding the dark with diamonds, rubies, pearls,
Occasional emeralds as the streetlights change
Keeping the sleeping people safe.
        Estranged
From the wild, dark, natural speaking world I ride.
This wooded ridge juts from the lights below,
A long black land of peace in a broad sea
Of massed humanity, where lights keep rules,
And laws abide to keep the people kind.
Here on the hill, a single, fitful gleam
Defines a welcome, warmth, and careful eyes
That probe me gently but respect my pride.

FALL WITH NO HARVEST

Should autumn come, and leaves hang limp and brown
Without the red and gold of harvest home,
And should the sun retreat behind the shroud
Of sodden Northwest skies as the year dies,
I would be forced to muse on final things,
Search under musky loam for sign of hope,
For seeds, small rodents, tiny insect life:
Light-powered life that lives in hope of spring.

Should sun retreat without a dying flame
At the day's end, the desultory rain
Absorbing colors into sodden grey,
And should the tangled orchard drop no gold
Of pear or sweet old apple, nor the blue of plum,
I would be forced to sharpen clippers and saws,
Climb into brittle branches, cut the dead wood,
Infertile waterspouts, until the trees
Are skeletal and clean, waiting to green.

Should the first freeze come early, bitter and deep,
Biting the tender plants to their tough rootstock,
Should freezing rains weigh down the trees with ice,
Tall poplars cracking with the report of guns,
I would be forced to build my winter fires
Of trash wood, prunings, scraps of old verse, and dreams,
Rise into friendless dark to feed my flocks,
Make a quick meal, retreat to winter work
Of mending, tending, coaxing sunlife from the fire
To illuminate my pruned and empty heart.

RESTLESS

Restless, tonight, I drive the winding road,
Swing round curves for solace, dancing through dark
To challenge all my senses, still my mind.
Yes, I have jobs to do, friends I hold dear
(Though solitude's not new), nor do I fear
Dark violence, but some nameless unease
Has drawn me from my homely evening fire
And drives me out into the windy night
To seek the answer to hidden desire.

What is not done? What duty's unfulfilled?
Whom have I slighted? Where am I meant to be?
I could walk all night, such restless energy
Drives my awareness with relentless goad.
Even unchallenged sexual appetite
And fantasy of dreams I have not willed
Suggest that somehow I must soon embark
Upon a venture of an unknown kind:
Unknown adventure, how you tug and tease,
Tempting my will to hazard, and to choose
A glorious challenge I cannot refuse.

DARK DAY

A dark day, struck with swords of sunlight;
Rain comes and goes, and comes again in clouds
Soft as the tears I might have shed, were I
To weep.
        The tears rise and sting: I blink
And rainbows blossom and the world is bright.

VI

POETS IN THE AGORA

Of Poets, Per Verse and Other Wise	73
Déja Vu—A Song for Satyricon	74
Cafe Oasis (September, 1984)	75
"Bill Stafford Says..." (Blue Heron Cafe, Portland, 1990)	76
Summer of '94	78
For Penny Avila	79
Going Home (For A Street Poet)	81
John's Poems	82
For Two Street Poets	83
Skyline Cafe	85
For a Poet Dying Unknown (Michael Speer 1933–1975)	86

OF POETS
PER VERSE AND OTHER WISE

Sappho, a Greek, was an outspoken lady
Who wrote lively verses extolling her love.
Her terms were explicit, and bound to elicit
A frown from the meek, who found her theme shady
Since it was a lady whose charms she sang of.

Elizabeth B, to a poet named Browning,
Recounted the Ways of Her Love for her guy:
An aerial passion, for such was the fashion
(No parts of his person enlivened her verse
So perhaps we assume that the fella was shy?)

Bard Willie the Great could grow wildly elated
Describing his passions for one young and fair.
His verses endure, although nobody's sure
Of whom he was prating—a lady-in-waiting?
Or was it a lad with a delicate air?

Now men through the ages have scribbled on pages
Descriptions of ladies they sought to possess:
The colors and size of their bosoms and eyes,
The fevers and rages provoked by the stages
Of feelings their words were too fine to confess.

I admit to elation at frank admiration,
My visual assets described with fond care,
But no inventory's an adequate story
(My mirror's no liar!)—you'll have to fly higher,
For all these will fade: let the buyer beware.

DÉJA VU—
A SONG FOR SATYRICON

The satyrs leap, the Muses muse
As each expresses "where he's at";
Mutter, mumble, shout or roar,
Grab the mike and hold the floor,
Sing the bard, miaou the cat
What do you dare, and what refuse?

I've seen this scene, I've viewed this view,
The theme's familiar, and the tune
Revolves the comic/tragic mask:
Cry out your pain, rhyme 'moon' with 'June'
Three thousand years of Déja Vu—

(At *least* that long, I'm sure it's true)
And nothing new? No shock in store?
No monumental, single task,
No music that does not sound flat,
No answer that I'm waiting for:
What do I dare? What can I lose?

I've had, you see, a Vuja day:
None of this ever occurred before!
My horoscope ran out of luck
(Rely on wits instead of pluck).
What's new's the view of the same old store
Once you have dared to throw it away
This Vuja Day.

CAFE OASIS
(SEPTEMBER, 1984)

Hurrah for young poets!—angry and unafraid
To sing their songs, to listen, share the floor,
To stand behind the verses they have made,
To feel, to pound the wall, to weep, to roar.

Bearded and bold, young poets face the old
Taunting their certainties, capitulations,
Circumstantial lies. Their songs unfold
Predictably, their grievances, elations,

Celebrations of the youth of flesh
Their condemnation of the compromise
Age makes with circumstance, the little deaths
That sap the spirit of the cautious wise.

Hurrah for young poets, singing their earnest truth:
Perennial as spring is the first strength of youth.

"BILL STAFFORD SAYS. . . ."
(BLUE HERON CAFE, PORTLAND, 1990)

The boy beside me on a counter stool,
In a good tweed jacket and a black beret,
Was young, full of himself, and very certain.
"Writing your daily poem?" he condescended.
"Mine is all done. I have to be alone—
I often use the Oriental Garden:
I like the ambience, you know, the peace.
My best, most precious thoughts have come from there."

I nodded, didn't lift my eyes, but he went on:
"Bill Stafford says he writes a poem a day,
Always and without fail—he's Poet Laureate—
He writes a poem a day, and so do I."
Undoubtedly, I thought, *Bill Stafford knows*
The catch in the throat at every poem's start,
Like swinging birches, it's that heady leap
Committing you to the experience,
No turning back, riding the poem down
In a leafy rush, not noticing the scratches
Till the earth rises to meet your feet, and you stand
Dazed and grateful, empty of all but air.

Another day, a bright young girl sat down:
"I never rewrite anything. My verse
Is not self-conscious, not, you know, contrived."
Her clothes proclaimed a studied attitude:
Colored scarves fluttered, her hands, her hair
Fluttered, and her scent was from the weed.
"It all comes pouring out: I talk in verse,
Sometimes, but not in rhyme: I just hate rhyme,
And William Stafford never rewrites things:
He says he never rewrites anything."

I murmured something about discipline,
And what it takes to test your every word
Until you know that it can take the weight
of your intention.
                      "That's contrived," she said.
"I'm passionate: I always speak right out."

I like Bill Stafford's verse. He's rooted here
As Frost was in New England. I suppose
He knows all that he needs of discipline:
The fluid ease of his line, the clean spare grace
Of unpretentious images—was learned.

A teaching poet's cautious, though he'll be quoted
Out of context, as above I've noted.

SUMMER OF '94

The wild Irish poets who liked to read in bars
are languishing in hospital for running into cars,
the followers of Stafford are now jostling for his place
Nuyorkians are everywhere and slam it in your face:
it's summertime in Portland, poets reading in the park,
The disaffected, unelected, waiting for the dark.

The fanciers of discipline are deemed to be old hat;
both rhyme and reason are ruled out; we're too advanced for that!
We must be multicultural, eclectic and ecstatic;
the very few disciples of The Classic seem erratic!

It's summertime in Portland, poets reading at the zoo—
just bring a scrap of paper there, and you can read it too.

FOR PENNY AVILA

MARCH 1992

Whose generous heart reaches out to street poets and children
Whose words of praise mean more than diamonds,
Whose steady hand has put up many a rider
Onto the winged steed of poetry,
Lie not now earthbound, shackled to pain,
But breathe deeply of his indomitable spirit
And rise again, whole, to mount your fiery steed
Great rider of that mighty Pegasus.

SEPTEMBER 1993

Who praised my reading at the Riverway,
      remembering my name,
Who took me down to Kesey's ranch with Walt,
      knowing that I would care,
Invited me to read before the Governor,
and summoned me to visit her at home
to give things that gave a direful hint
before the surgery she told nobody of;
to whom I wrote when it was just too brash
to think of coming to the hospital
as though I mattered in her busy life
      (I never thought I did),
whose phone calls always livened up my heart
inviting me to share her trip abroad,

sharing her tales of travel afterward
because I couldn't come, and urging me
to travel soon because our lives are short—

Oh, Penny, what a friend you were to me,
your good opinion making me so proud
to have so kind a friend, so generous,
so full of courage. How I miss you now,
and how I wish that I'd had more to give.
A little bird, some home-made bread and jam . . .
I've copies of ten letters that I sent
to you, but your replies were spoken words,
kind deeds, and now, in memory, your love.

—with love, from Elizabeth

GOING HOME
(FOR A STREET POET)

There's his two boys
And there's his brother,
And there once was Marge
But she came to the end
Of putting up with him.

Summer's a good time
For living in the park;
Just take that check for disability
And give it to the priest
To hold.
And the bus ticket, too.

Pick up a lot of empties in the park,
And turn them in for cash;
Sell blood, eat at MacDonald's
Dumpster.
Sometimes a buddy buys a drink:
A guy can get along.

Oh yeah, you gotta have clean clothes
And something for the kids.
Just put them in a bag—
And get a friend to hold them
Till you go.

At summer's end
It's getting cold:
Time to go home.
(It's where they got to take you in,
Says Robert Frost.)

JOHN'S POEMS

Blarney tongue, cadged coffee,
Begged a cigarette
Asked for help in typing his poems
Because he had no cash.

The poems?
They got lost
Or stolen
Anyhow they're gone.

Well, he was drunk, you see.
How could he tell
What happened to his poems?
It was the day
His "Disability" came in,
The check they partied on.

So now he's broke again
And gone to sell some blood:
Big man, he's got a lot of it,
And shit, and fucking language,
And, sometimes,
King James.

FOR TWO STREET POETS

A pair of Celtic troubadours—
Two errant knights of Poetry—
Both wed to Lady Alcohol
Desert her, now and then,
And tipsily or soberly
Indulge themselves romantically,
Flirt with the Muse of Poetry
Ignoring pompous protocol
And gloriously, grandiosely,
Takes up, each, his pen:

Irreverently bawdy bard,
The one, with gruff, incisive wit
Depicts The Street with all its grit,
Tells tales of ladies soft and hard,
Reduces Shakespeare's greatest hit
To seven lines or ten.

The other, with King Jamesian rage
And gorgeous language, treats our ears
To images of earthly horrors,
Feasts of dogs and hells of sorrows,
Angels fierce and human tears
On every crumpled page.

They celebrate our common Muse,
The universe, the common man,
The dreams of glory, love, and pain.
The urge to sing, the glorious plan.
Whatever images they use
Or substances they may abuse,

They're Poets first, and it's our gain
Spellbound to hear Bad George recite
Or John propose to fight.

Today they knew I was alone
And had been ill and sorrow bound.
They called me on the telephone
With kind nonsense and gallantry
And teased each other foolishly
With silly jokes and bawdy jeers
And made me laugh away my tears . . .

Whatever earth they walk upon—
It's holy ground.

SKYLINE CAFE

A countryside cafe, where he and she
Divide the work: he cooks, she tends the till.
They know their customers by name: they see
Some of them every day, and coffee comes
The moment I sit down. I sip and write.
The washer roars, the ventilator hums
(The old ice-cream machine won't last the night).
Over the clanks and roars, the radio
Tuned to a station I can't get at home
Plays music, pops from twenty years ago.

Nowhere is the Muse more like to come.
My pen moves smoothly almost without my will
No interruption, telephone, doorbell.
There's nowhere else on earth I write as well.

FOR A POET DYING UNKNOWN
(MICHAEL SPEER 1933–1975)

The senseless violence that took your life
Was not the greatest wrong: the murderer
Who put three bullets in your brain, the wife
Who took your son and all your heart with her,

Robbed you directly of past, present, and dream—
But those who lost the poems that you gave
Took more than these did from you. What can redeem
That earthly life that lasts beyond the grave?

What we who knew your friendship can recall
Is finite, dies with us: your loyalty,
Your trust, your search for God, your vision—all
Were in the poems you honed from love and pity.

Now we, who had these gifts, gather your song
To give you to this world, where you belong.

VII
ANTIC HUMORS

Dead Language   89

Canning Season   90

George in February   91

Fowl Language   93

A Fable   94

On Pushing Up Daisies   96

DEAD LANGUAGE

Our Latin teacher, with her bone-white skin,
Black hair and cold, grey eyes,
Swept into class the first day in a flowing cloak
Of scarlet.
"Salvete, Discipuli!" she trumpeted.
We were impressed.

The next day, awed and dignified,
We waited for her entrance quietly.
Who was this lively red-haired witch
Swirling a cloak of black?
Her eyes seemed green today—
and was it she?

On Wednesday she appeared in blue,
Her brilliant cloak was echoed in her eyes,
Her face now framed in golden curls.
Thursday was her brunette day,
And Friday she was silver.

We never missed her class
and learned to speak
a dead language.

CANNING SEASON

Of all fruit, peach is the most lascivious,
Juicy and sweet, slippery, easy to bruise.
In the beginning when God first made us
And turned to sister Eve, did he then use
The model of a ripe and rosy peach
For that first tender bottom, firm and round?
And Adam, whose own seat was out of reach
Of eyesight, thought the view profound
Of Eve, face down, asleep on Eden's grass,
Who, when she rose and faced his astonished eyes
Could not imagine why he gazed (that new-made lass)
At breasts like peaches of a smaller size.
For her, of course, the universe was new:
For him, she was a more than peachy view.

GEORGE IN FEBRUARY

I have a neighbor who likes to run around bare,
used to live down the road and up a long curving drive
outta sight, like, you know: you'd have to drive up to his house
before you might be surprised, first, at his door
by a little boy tot who'd forgot to put on his clothes
grinning at you. As you smiled at his upturned face
your eyes lost their focus: two hairy feet, very brown,
framed your view of the child, and a a pair of brown shins
and more, and more of him, all in a uniform shade
of very brown skin all the way to his hair (which is thin).

Is he making a statement, and putting you down for your clothes
and showing he isn't afraid of your judgment, and he
is more natural and honest than we? Could be. Maybe.
People who lived in the neighborhood somehow forgot
to warn any newcomer how they were going to find George. . . .

Now he's built a new house on the lot in the woods behind mine
and it seems that he likes to come visiting, though to be fair
he's taken to phoning ahead to make sure that I'm home
and nobody shockable's there.

Today as I came from the barn after doing the chores
there was George on the phone, and did I have bread to sell?
(Sure thing.) And did I have guests? (Well, no, not today.)
I was starting my breakfast, and there stood my honest friend,
no mistaking him, there he was in his skin, all of him, brown.
Now it's one thing to walk clad in sunshine in summer: today

I was wearing my woolies because there was frost on the ground.
I hadn't yet lit the wood fire, having come, as I said,
from the barn.

                Well, two can make statements, you know, and so—
I put on the kettle for coffee and offered him some
and talked about neighborhood politics, and who would run
for political office, just neighborly gossip, you know.
He stayed for an hour or more, talking faster and faster,
slowly congealing in spite of the coffee, but not
giving up. If there's one thing my neighbor always enjoys,

It's making statements.

FOWL LANGUAGE

Out by the barn, all the speech is foul:
A cacophony of squeak and howl
And bark and honk and neigh and bray,
And each sound certain what it means to say.

Even a hen doesn't need much luck
To communicate exactly with a squawk and cluck,
Yet if you notice what a hen must endure
You won't be surprised that her words aren't pure.

"Bick! Bick! Bick!" she calls her chick
To eat a special goody and to get there quick.
At butchering time, when her luck runs out,
"Pluck-a-duck! Pluck-a-duck!" you'll hear her shout.

And for all emergencies, her whole life through,
She uses dirty language: it's the thing to do.
When the cock dances up with his long, curved spurs
The hen runs, shouting back an age-old curse:

"Fuck! fuck-fuck, fuck-fuck, fuck-fuck!"
The hen protests. "Fuck-a-duck! Fuck-a-duck!"
When she's tucked her egg in the secret hay,
"Tuck-a-raw, tuck-tuck!" you will hear her say.

When you search for an egg in the nest-box straw
A ruffled hen gives a sleepy "Awwww,"
But a broody hen with a family planned
Will shout "Fuck OFF!" and peck your hand.

Odd that in the speech of modern men
They needs must employ the curse of a hen.
When there's clean, specific language, good for all intents,
A dumb cluck's curse is the word man vents!

A FABLE

Janet Jones was a practiced sinner
Who thought of men as she thought of dinner:
The hearty sort, to be wolfed right down,
The wit, to be teased with provoking frown.
She savored and tasted: stewed or fried
No end to the dishes Janet tried.
No doubt about it: men were a habit
(As some are enamored of sauteed rabbit).

To face the issue and make no bones
About what happened to Miss Janet Jones:
One day, in pursuing her avid taste
She met a young man who was quite straitlaced!
She fed him well and she treated him right
But he would not satisfy her appetite.
He pleased her eyes, but it ended there,
So she planned his seduction with the greatest care.

He arrived on time with flowers and books
And fed her a host of soulful looks.
Her wits at an end, her hopes betrayed,
Literary conversation was all they made,
And Janet Jones from her last wild tryst
Emerged a hardened sentimentalist.
No more does she wolf the young men down
And her eyes have developed a myopic frown,

For he fed her Shelley, and he fed her Keats,
Thomas, Eliot, and sundry other treats.
As her taste grew keen, her craving quicker
She read and read and grew steadily sicker.
It was the end of her healthy appetite,
For she married the man, and they read at night.

Janet Jones Brown grew old and lean,
And all that she craved was Ovaltine.

ON PUSHING UP DAISIES

The flesh of ancient dinosaurs,
Distilled by time, moves motor cars,
But Man in egoistic zeal
Consigns his body to cold steel
Denying to posterity
The juice of his mortality.

Who knows but what our myriad cells
Are thus confined to separate hells,
Denied an access to the earth
Which might have given them rebirth?
To come again as violets
Is no occasion for regrets.

VIII
TIME GONE

Time and the Pipe   99

Adam's Fallacy   100

Old Pictures   101

Helen of Troy

    Helen's Song   102

    Menelaus   103

    Paris   104

    Troy   105

Centaurs   106

TIME AND THE PIPE

It is not Time that flies, but rather, we
Hurry through Time, wasting mortality,
And garner nothing of the fruit we planned
Because we do not stop to understand:

Harvest is never home! Time is not ripe!
We wait in vain for Pan's immortal pipe
To summon us away from toil and care,
Finding at last, he pipes the empty air.

And as we reach again, with greedy clutch
At love and life, which fade beneath the touch,
We hear, over the gains no one enjoyed,
Pan's evil laughter at the fruit destroyed.

ADAM'S FALLACY

Adam's first fallacy was naming names,
Insisting on particularity,
Defining terms, making his puny claims
To Eden's treasure, though it was given free.

And Eve, enchanted by the names he'd speak,
By his excitement in the new-made earth,
And his conviction that she was unique,
Joined in the game, as midwife to the birth

Of Ego. And the first sin of Eve was this:
Gifted with sensual wisdom, yet she denied
All that she knew of simple, wordless bliss,
To prate of Good and Evil for her pride.

Had they not thought this was indeed The Tree,
They could have eaten apples harmlessly.

OLD PICTURES

Old pictures, brown with age, are your delight.
"That's Aunt Christine, my mother, and my dad,
My Gramma Plass, Gran'pop, my little sis—
And that's my little brother."
                                        Dad, that's you—
Your little self, when you were very small.
You never had a brother, though you wanted one,
And hoped you'd find that friendship in a son.

The child sits comfortably, close to the knee
Of the sweet-faced lady with the silver hair.
The parents' look is stern, the little girl
Is querulous. Only the older lady
And the little boy are safe in love.
(Do you recall the warmth of that friendly skirt
As contrast to the starch of your Sunday shirt?)

(No. 3, from "Five for My Father, at Ninety")

HELEN OF TROY

HELEN'S SONG

Tonight my flesh is pink and tan
Where the light warms, or shadows fall.
How among men can I find a man
To love and honor over all?

When the light dims and shadows sway
All of the eyes are greedy, stark.
I hide my arms and turn away:
The prophecy is dark, is dark!

Cursed with this flesh, once a delight,
And cursed with awareness of my fate,
I tremble on fame's uneasy height
Certain to fall by my body's weight.

Made by the gods, an artifact,
Love is not mine to gain or give:
How shall I keep my heart intact?
How can I live, but never live?

MENELAUS

My husband's arms were dark and strong
And I walked in his house with my hair unbound.
Laughing at fate, I feared no wrong,
Convinced that my dream could not be found.

Paris, a shepherd, came to me—
A solemn queen in a place of state—
Singing of Love's nobility
Stirring a longing known too late.

He made demands he did not speak,
Implying only the gift he'd give:
He was the dream I dared not seek,
His love the life that I longed to live.

Scorning responsibility,
He moved my heart to his care-less way.
In love with the joy that seemed so free,
Turning, I bid my shepherd stay.

PARIS

Paris would have me a laughing child,
Ever a nymph by the sounding stream,
Free as Oenone, love-beguiled
Gift of the goddess, living dream.

Thought of my home and the prophecies
Fled with my prayer in the ritual smoke;
Fear of the future, law's decrees
Vanished like flame when the goddess spoke.

Men will condone as "goddess-driven"
The flight from duty to delight,
Laying that when love's gift is given
Wrong is not wrong, and right not right.

What of Oenone, tears grown cool
Mourning her love who has come to me?
What of the Grecian vengeance cruel?
What . . .
        of the end of ecstacy?

TROY

Paris, so young in carefree pride
Lies dead in the city we helped destroy.
Moored in a ship on the restless tide
I wept in the wind that blew from Troy.

My careless dream led to this care:
Guilt for the death I should not bewail,
Smoke in the wind on my tangled hair,
Cries of the dead on my festal veil.

Pride of the Greeks, men called me proud
When, as a girl, I hid my fear,
Knowing that love was not allowed,
Knowing my choice was hard and clear.

Sadly, I chose where honor led:
Wealth, to protect my beauty's bane
Till Paris stained the hostess bed,
Brought me to joy and back again.

CENTAURS

The centaurs run with slender, flashing limbs
Across the souls of men:
Their delicate, terrible, tearing hooves
Cut to the quick and leave revealed
What lies within.
Their molten eyes look deep into the hearts
And minds of simple men,
Knowing the restless, fierce desires,
Knowing the search for quiet calm
At constant war.
The centaurs arch their aching human frames
And eagerly toss their legs,
Stretch, longing to rend themselves,
Be man or beast—be one, at peace.

IX
ENVOI

Audience With an Olympian   109

AUDIENCE WITH AN OLYMPIAN

Needing compassion, we sought the height,
And there, to her face, we told the tale,
Seeking no help: No one can give
Help to a mortal who has to live.
We must have looked distraught and pale—
The goddess was weeping.
                        We hoped she might.

Afterword

VOICES

I

"I took Elizabeth to the hospital one day to an appointment," Jean Bradley relates, "and returned to pick her up a couple hours later. She was not yet back in the waiting area, so I asked at the nurses' station for her whereabouts. Imagine my surprise at the response: 'Who? There's no Elizabeth Bolton on this morning's schedule.' Our expressions mirrored mutual blank incomprehension for a few seconds, until Elizabeth emerged just down the hall and cheerily called, 'She's looking for me!'—'Well . . . goodbye, Ms. de Lackner,' said the nurse. Looking at me askance once more, she returned to her duties. Sic transit revelation!"

Thus it was that some knew "only" Elizabeth Bolton, while those who had shared decades-long friendship with Barbara de Lackner knew "both"— a clearly impossible semantic distinction, as the two were quite inseparable. BdeL arrived "first," however—via Scarsdale, New York, then west to Texas, then college variously at Dennison, Columbia, Pomona, Stanford, and San Francisco State. Married in the mid 1950s, she and her husband resided in Claremont, CA while he finished graduate school. Both started out as teachers, BdeL of middle-school English and drama, her husband of high school theater and English. Even in those early Claremont days, she had began to develop a notably effective and highly original, drama-based curriculum.

The couple then made one of those life-directing decisions and moved to their property on Willapa Bay, site of the summer camp called Sherwood Forest, where BdeL's husband had spent happy childhood and teenage years. They made a commitment: to make it once again a special place and experience for children. For the next twenty or so years, no matter how their individual paths might alter or diverge, Sherwood remained the nexus of their lives. As the camp's codirector, BdeL managed an unpredictable array of responsibilities, including overseeing the kitchen, which in some seasons fed as many as forty staff and campers at each meal, and keeping close watch over the infirmary. She also continued to improve and refine her drama method, helping young campers find their voices and confidence as they framed their ever-constant, ever-changing, annual "Robin Hood" play. For diversion, she tamed a succession of fledgling crows she commissioned her oldest son to bring her—first Charlie, Hombre next, then the notorious Brouha, then Chico. . . . The birds stayed a while, to the campers' delight (and occasional annoyance), then grew up to resume their crow-lives with the local flock, but were never far away.

The family finally settled, during the school year, at Hill Farm above Portland. There they raised three children, a variable assortment of chickens, goats, ducks, sheep, geese, guinea fowl, cats, Sheltie dogs, sometimes a horse or two, and a substantial garden.

Sadly, the marriage eventually ended, and with it, the unique teamwork and life of which Sherwood had been both center and orbit. BdeL/EB returned to Hill Farm where, though sometimes painfully and with difficulty, she determined that hard work, deep spiritual conviction, and the will to succeed in her own terms would not fail her resolve to live a fully aware life. She turned inward to the writing that had always sustained her, and then, as she had only infrequently done before, outward to forge new friendships, new professional contacts, and enduring connections with writers of the Northwest; she became one of their number.

Thus it was that EB came into her own a little over twenty years ago. "Why 'Elizabeth Bolton'?" some of us quizzed BdeL persistently at the time. "What's wrong with your own name?" True, as always, to her nature—humor and mischief not least—and never one to answer a direct question directly, eventually she revealed that EB was her paternal great-grandmother, a woman of great intelligence, forbearance, and kindness, who was highly esteemed by her large family. Perhaps in this way, BdeL expressed her love and respect for the name's first bearer. (They also shared, across four generations, an uncanny resemblance.)

EB is far more than a persona, far more than an act or device—though at times, BdeL would mischievously declare: "I can't do that sort of thing [read at Satyricon? at the zoo? hang out with Portland's street poets?]—but EB can!" EB is, thus, an independent being who speaks with her own voice. One can say that she succeeded in becoming both the sojourner and the journey itself.

—LORNA PRICE

II

I first met Barbie at Sherwood Forest Camp when I was thirteen. . . . She had a highly developed sixth sense . . . especially if a person was going through a difficult time. Her way was always gentle. . . . She didn't tell others what to do, but simply made suggestions, and in her suggestions, helped us understand a bit more about each other's humanity.

I hear Barbie's voice in the way I speak to my cats. . . . I see the way she held her head to one side, the delight in her eyes at seeing me happy, and more than all these, the sparkle that flashed and twinkled in her eyes. . . . Her last words to me were: "It is a pity people think identity matters, when it turns out that love is the only thing that matters." She certainly gave away a lot of it.

—VIRGINIA RAYMOND MAXAM

III

One summer, I cooked at camp. I seem to recall those and other times with Barbie in scenes and vignettes, which leaves me wondering if she staged many moments of her life: Barbie sitting in the sun on the Ark's deck, laughing, surrounded by camper friends, spinning tales and spinning wool from her own sheep. Skeins of yarn dyed by hand with home-made dyes drape the rail, their earthy tones blending with the silver greys of the deck wood and pale green moss hanging from trees . . . bright colors in her carefully crafted wild garden. Brown gulls, white gulls, and a crow grab shellfish at the shore. The birds soar nearly straight up, pause, drop their prey onto the rocks to crack them open, then plunge to seize their exposed dinner. The crow probably descends from one Barbie tamed years earlier, which became a camp hanger-on and general pest. He went from stealing from the gulls' beach bombardments to staging his own, then teaching the trick to other crows.

After chores, Barbie nabs me and we race, laughing boisterously, to beat the older campers and staff to the best canoe. I don't know a thing about paddling a canoe. Barbie is expert. She takes the bow and motions me to the stern. Soon she has shaped us into a team. And we almost fly over the sparkling water, wind and sun burning our cheeks.

At Hill Farm, she once talked me through a close encounter with half-a-dozen bossy geese. "You need to act like you're an even bigger goose than they are." She chortled, cupped her hands into her armpits, and flapped her arms. She looked as if she were performing the Oktoberfest "Chicken" dance. It worked.

A friend once said we are the keepers of each other's histories. Strong and enduring friendships contain legacies that blur the edges of that finality we call death.
—RUTH AUSTEN

IV

Barbie was a huge influence on my life, and I lived month-to-month on the power of four summer weeks at camp.... [Yet] in all honesty, she made me deeply uncomfortable at times, even as a child. She was so often in a world that had little bearing on the world as I existed in it.

I went to Hill Farm after her death to help Susie [her daughter] reclaim the hard drive on Barbie's computer. We discovered her personal calendar, and on every day she had typed: "Today I am cancer-free...." Today, I see it as the perfect example of all that Barbie was. She was the only person

[I know of] in the world . . . who could believe she would make a thing so, just by willing it. I think she believed it even as she died. . . . It is this grace that she most imparted to me as a child and an adult: There are things that should exist in this world that do not, and it is our job to believe in them until they do.

—CATHERINE RONDTHALER

LORNA PRICE, an editor and writer, lives in Friday Harbor, Washington.

VIRGINIA RAYMOND MAXAM, a teacher and artist, and CATHERINE RONDTHALER, an artist, are former Sherwood campers; each lives in Portland, Oregon.

RUTH AUSTEN, a writer and journalist, breeds and raises Arabian sporthorses in Banning, California, and now cares for BdeL's Arab mare, Bonnie.

ACKNOWLEDGMENTS

Grateful acknowledgment is made of publications in which some of these poems first appeared:

Bay Area Poets Coalition (Deserted Wife, Dead Language)
Calapooya Collage (Of Poets Per Verse and Other Wise)
CPRS Ridgerunner (Fog Zen)
Eclectic Muse (Willapa Bay Before Dawn, Requiem for a Cathedral)
From the Lost Corner (Willapa Bay Before Dawn, Catastrophes)
OSPA Assemblage (Dead Crow by the Roadside)
Paper Boats Review (Time and the Pipe)
Peace Gazette (Peace)
Plains Poetry Journal (Time and the Pipe, Peace)
Poets' Sanctuary (On Pushing Up Daisies)
Poetspeak (Fog Zen, On Pushing Up Daisies)
Pointed Circle (Fog Zen)
Riverway Assemblage (The Logic of the Heart, Canning Season, Peace)
Satyricon Assemblage II (Adam's Fallacy)
Satyricon Assemblage (Peace, An Illness [Epiphany])
South Park Journal (Trapped Fox, Requiem for a Cathedral,
  A Caprice of Capricorns)
Street Poets (For Two Street Poets)
Talapus Anthology (Requiem for a Cathedral)
Words on the Wind, Vulgaris (Requiem for a Cathedral,
  An Illness [Epiphany])

INDEX OF TITLES

A Fable	94
Adam's Fallacy	100
Archetypes:	
Grandfathers	38
Dad	39
Mother	39
Audience with an	
Olympian	107
"Bill Stafford Says..."	
(Blue Heron Cafe,	
Portland, 1990)	76
Breakthrough	52
Cafe Oasis	
(September 1984)	75
Canning Season	90
Caprice of Capricorns	25
Catastrophes	26
Centaurs	106
Christmas Elk	28
Dark Day	70
Dead Language	89
Dead Crow by	
the Roadside	63
Déja vu	74
Deposition	55
Deserted Wife	62
Epiphany	49
Fall With No Harvest	68
Farm Chores During	
the Drought	17
First Things	54
First Day of Spring	
(March 22, 1991)	15
Fog Zen	16
For A Poet Dying Unkown	
(Michael Speer 1933–1975)	86
For Dad	42
For Feliz	29
For My Filly, Dead	30
For My Mother	43
For My Parents	41
For Penny Avila	79
For the Living Children	44
For Two Street Poets	83
For Wiyanna	
(October 7, 1997)	20
Fowl Language	93
George in February	91
Going Home	
(For a Street Poet)	81
Grandchild	
(for Amara)	46
Helen of Troy:	
Helen's Song	102
Menelaus	103
Paris	104
Troy	105

Hill Farm	65	Skyline Cafe	85
Hostage	45	Skyline Drive—Sunset	66
		Snowy Owls on	
John's Poems	82	Grassy Island	33
		Solitude and Purpose	51
Lost Farm	13	Summer of '94	78
		Synchronicity	37
Nanna's Hats	40	Thanksgiving 1979,	
		Remembered	18
Of Poets Per Verse		Thanksgiving	
and Other Wise	73	Meditation, 1983	67
Of Thought and Reality	58	The Logic of the Heart	56
Old Pictures	101	Time and the Pipe	99
On Pushing Up Daisies	96	Trapped Fox	32
On Receiving the Gift of			
Five Peacocks	34	Unmeeting Wishes	57
Peace	50	Willapa Bay Before Dawn	22
		Winter Song	61
Red Vixen	31		
Requiem for a Cathedral	14		
Restless	69		